SCIENTIFIC POETRY

by

Madeline Goldstein

A Lyceum Book

Carlton Press, Inc.   New York, N.Y.

Dedicated to the memory of my geology advisor Dr. Leo Hall

CONTENTS

Introduction

The author of this poetry book is one of a few geologic poets in the United States. This collection of poems would be found within the School of Rational Poetry if there was such a school. The terminology of many of the poems is scientific.

I attended many universities, and I met people whom I wanted to preserve as poetic fossils. Each poem about an individual serves to preserve that person in history the way I perceived that person to be. This poetry collection expresses the honest feelings of a young woman scientist. In this lifetime, I was in search of true and genuine people. Many of the individuals found and described were exemplary virtuous people though some were disappointing. Each must have a place in history, nonetheless, as I decided to write their poems.

Science has the potentiality to be poetic. There are elements of science which can make a poem more meaningful and interesting. I value a poem which is reasoned more than a poem which seems to be nonsense. A scientist carefully observes objects and subjects, then describes them. A poem which contains fine details about a subject is more interesting than a vague poem. In order to write a detailed poem a poet must observe a subject carefully. Scientific poems are written about what is real. A scientific poem is internally consistent.

The biographical sketches are more meaningful to me because scientific terminology was used in several instances. Geologic and chemical terminology can be used meaningfully to describe people, because people have many attributes which rocks and chemicals have. Many of the processes which geologic materials and chemicals go through people also go through, e.g. weathering, reacting, developing faults (in many cases). People are living earth and so are intrinsically geologic. There are so many chemical reactions happening inside of us each moment that we are also intrinsically chemical. Use of scientific terminology to describe a person can have a humorous effect.

The opening astronomical poem explains the special relation of man to God and Angels. The author believes Angels and God evolved before man as organizations of energy. Because energy moves faster than matter, it evolves faster. Man evolved later as an organization of matter and energy. Intelligence, whether of matter or energy, is believed by the author to be a product of evolution initially. This poem also discusses the origin and future of the universe.

In the future the universe can look forward to more big bangs as the initiation of a cycle, more galaxy formation and destruction. Though expansion occurs in some places today, contraction occurs in other regions of the universe. Our solar system is just one part of the universe. The author believes there is life on many planets in our galaxy and other galaxies. A lifeform made of energy is favoured on certain planets because such a lifeform wouldn't care about the chemical composition of the atmosphere. There might be stars and planets inhabited only by Angels because the atmosphere isn't hospitable for other life. Our evolution is being watched.

The object of the author's love is variously described as a crystallized mineral, a rock formation with human characteristics, and a planet. Science comes to life in this poetry collection. One of the poems uses the image of the author's love as a geosyncline full of sentiments. If a man's love was as constant as the facets on a crystal, the poet's love would last for eternity.

Many of the people who were described are professors; some are famous people. I wish to thank everyone who posed for me so I could paint their portrait with words.

Madeline Goldstein

SCIENTIFIC POETRY

The Essence of God

God is made of energy in reality
So He can flow through matter easily.
His energy is organized in a definite form,
So He can think infinitely long.

God evolved from energy that was free,
As energy was attracted to energy, you see.
He evolved with Angels less powerful than He,
At a time long before Man came to be.

When big bangs set energy free,
It can make forms much higher than we.
Too much matter or too much energy,
In one place makes bangs happen,
Then energy cools and galaxies shapen.

Matter crystallizes as energy slows.
Particles join to form atoms.
Some particles which form at temperatures high,
Will decay at temperature low.

Massless particles form part of God.
Photons join with photons,
To make a pattern that is bright.
God has the appearance of living light.
Gamma rays and x-rays also must be there,
As photons decompose in the air.

God can travel at the speed of light.
We are slow beings in his sight.
The Angels travel just as fast.
They will guide us when the time is right,
Sweep us up as energy fields in their light.
Carry us far to where it's safe
To begin again the human race.

Each person has a spirit made of energy.
The best of us have one in harmony.
The atoms inside our brain
Serve as a template for a field of energy.
The worst of our fields will merely dissipate.
They learned to care for people too late.
The best of us have a field that can go very far,
Reaching out to a star.

Processes go on eternally in many cases.
Evolution is repeated again and again.
There are people out there somewhere,
In distant galaxies on equivalent planets,
Waiting for us to take notice.
If only our spaceships could travel far,
Outside our corner of the universe.

One bang, two bangs, there'll be more I'm sure,
Or all stars would be from fewer galaxies.
As billions of galaxies are known to exist,
There must have been repeated action,
To make many explosions.

The universe is and always will be.
For eternity cycles always shall happen.
Though expansion occurs in some place today,
Contraction occurs in another.
As matter and energy are attracted,
Why should expansion always be,
Of matter across the universal sea?
There must have been contraction,
For a big bang ever to be.

There always was energy somewhere,
As something cannot come from nothing, I swear.
Though energy merely needs to slow to beome matter,
Matter must have something added to become the former.

Somewhere antimatter is organizing in the air.
There are antimatter creatures, so beware.
Antimatter people might also be peaceful,
But touch their hand and you're not there.
The same amount of antimatter exists as matter,
Since massless particle decay can't produce,
One without the other.
Each predominates in some place,
Due to dispersion caused by explosion.
We're over here, they're over there;
The two shall rarely meet.
God didn't mean for us often to greet.

A Geologic Love Poem

I love you more by far
Than the myriad of stars
That twinkle brightly across the sky,
As much as all the meteors
That have fallen along a solitary path,
Trying to reach their destination.
Like a comet's tail,
I follow you far away,
Captured like a satellite in orbit,
Safe inside its course.

You are an unusual planet,
Like none ever seen before,
Spiritual, spinning at a high angle,
Through the heavens.
Physical, composed of rocks and minerals,
Well formed and crystalline.
Pleasing in all three dimensions,
Ahead of your time,
By hundreds of thousands of years.
A geologic projection of history,
In possession of knowledge not understood.

One day perhaps if good and true,
I will fall to you,
Held tight by warm solid earth,
Compassionate from head to foot.
Not to be vaporized,
In a vacuous atmosphere,
Impacting on uncaring ground.
One with strong lips,
Rising as a border of firm earth,
Around your mouth.

My love for you is larger
Than the moon's smile,
When the sun shines.
As vast as the entire universe.
Like a sun providing energy,
Inside a personal universe,
You radiate inside my mind.
Make me feel warm and cared for,
When alone.

You are the highest educated planet,
That I see.
Beneath you, I sit, a Pluto next to Jupiter,
A Mars next to Saturn.
So learned a person pleases me merely to hear,
Some ancient secrets of how to cure.
Though we may never be physically near,
In my mind, I love you sure.

You are 4.6 billion years; I am 3.4—
Two beings destined to meet late,
An elderly man, a young woman.
So what, that's the score.
I'd try you out,
If you were millions more.

Was I produced from your rib,
The Pacific Ocean,
Or did you capture me,
One fine morning?
There you were one day,
Sitting behind a large desk,
Right in front of me,
And here I was in love with you.

Attracted like a magnet,
To its corresponding pole.
Oriented towards you,
Like a point fixed in space.
Unable to move or love,
In another direction.

You are truly a rare crystal,
Whose atoms are internally ordered,
In a genuine fashion.
Habits are of conservative tradition.
Tetra-triclinic,
Prismatic and charismatic.
Subhedral with one face,
Bilaterally symmetrical,
Shiny and lovable.
With seven planes of symmetry,
For each healing specialty.
A center of symmetry,
Which reflects a field,
In two directions.

You formed from solution paradoxically,
By raising the temperature and pressure.
Then the solution became sufficiently concentrated,
To produce a crystal of your intensity.
Before then atoms were free to move,
In all directions chaotically.
After then they were fixed and arranged,
As a crystalline mass, your body.

Shoulders are broad and tabular,
Profile is smooth and regular.
Handsome in internal configuration,
Though plain in external morphology,
Rarely do crystals present
An ideally shaped geometry.

More stable at higher energy levels
Than most people,
A vital lively mineral,
With just strong bonds,
Resulting in no cleavage along edges.

A soft mineral at heart,
Beneath outer firm layers,
With very great heat capacity,
Undergoing thermal expansion readily;
Have sensitive reactivity.
Go into a state of partial solution,
From hearing sad stories.

A trapezohedron,
Resulting from a three-fold axis,
Combined with two normal
Two-fold axes.
Scaling limits of the medical profession,
Like a real scalenohedron.
Arms and legs approximately tetragonal,
Trunk and waist hexagonal.
Your face is where it was most probable.
A unit cell is extended and differentiated
Throughout your body.

Your head is a C axis,
With two-fold symmetry.
Your arms at normal are A's and B's.
At the center of your palm,
Is your most distinguishing factor,
As a man—a five-fold hand.

You could be turned at short notice,
To show two halves equally desirable.
Your Miller Index is (111)
As it is fundamental.
With a goniometer,
I could locate you anywhere,
By equal angles between equivalent faces.

You are an open form,
Growing from encounters,
With other atoms,
In several directions.
Mainly parallel to planes,
With few lattice points.
Makes adding to a face
An easier case.

Perhaps it is my nature
To want to have
So excellent a crystal
In my collection.
Able to be gazed at
Only upon a desk.
Mesmerized by brilliant glitter,
But separated by thick glass,
As owned and valued,
By another crystallographer.

Maybe all have to settle someday
But not right now.
You are a crystal held inside my mind,
Unusual in internal quality,
With facets that never change.

All other crystals are defective,
Next to the class of your system.
Some lack any internal arrangement,
And are amorphous mineraloids.
Others can't be classified.

My Love For You

My love is like a fossilized endearment,
A Pleistocene fish; a wish for you.
It's something like great oceans that once spread
Over continents, surging with truth to be brought to be.
It brings a new day for you and for me.

My love tells of ancient movements.
It does what I haven't the words to say.
The Earth rules my love but, it also comes from above.
While I lie here thinking of what I can do for you,
I think of The Laws and how they will see us through.

My love is like a vast geosyncline,
Gently warped by ocean ways.
It's filled with fine layered sediments of you,
And stratified clays of lonely days and wanting you.
With deep rifts and faulted uplifts of past loves untrue.

Decayed matter smoulders within my midst,
From evolutive possibilities that did not last.
Heated and pressured my mind has become,
From thousands of pounds of thoughts,
Of what I wish to happen.

Compressed and pressured are we together.
Inside the temperature builds with time.
Outside the noise begins to roar.
Boulders crash and rush past one another.
Slowly we rise with changes brought forth by time,
By laws that can't be beat.
The Laws will break us and remake us.
Though distortions must be borne,
I swear it will be worth it evermore.
Memories split and thoughts collide,
Leaving us metamorphosed and fused.
Crystallized remnants we will become,
Of how love was meant to be.

How I'm Crabby For You

Baby crabs waddle below,
Shell pieces are tossed as their little legs go.
Instinct tells them what they should know.
Big crabs can't be told where to go.

Giant fights break arms in two.
And little fights lead to bigger fights,
Till a crab is left to think, what else can I do.

Some crabs pick on other crabs.
I try to stray away alone.
Then a big blue point crab comes along. That's you—
To keep this crab at home.

Little fights start then bigger fights.
Mean shells turn green.
Seaweed grows between them,
Till each is covered by a screen.

Each wanders 'cross shells and sea bells.
Their innocent crab-love stays hidden within.
Two little crab hearts;
Their innocent crab eyes
Try to take the other in.

But they're afraid their little arms are too thin,
And big claws don't hold well,
(A tight squeeze at best)
But crabs know what crabs must know,
That love isn't always the best show.
Though sand grains enter their mouth when they kiss,
They feel crab-love is bliss!

With little crab feelers, they sort out each other,
And choose a pole to rest.
A boy watches as I try to look my best.
He comes slowly down with a net.
And takes my blue point crab for a pet!

The Invertebrate Paleontology Professor

Last night while studying in my apartment,
I was inspired to write your description.
It took more than one type of fossil,
For your representation.

Face is shaped like that of a blastoid,
With radial cheek plates and deltoid forehead,
Lancet plated smile.
Wears a cosmopolitan expression,
Like fossils that have seen many places.
Diversity in plate arrangement,
Helps to keep students' interest.
Sometimes wears brachial and radial plates,
To appear unconventional.
Shirt is bordered by collar cells,
Suit is plaid and fits well.
Is colonial but stands also as an individual.

Pentremite delivering classical lectures,
Characterized by flexabilia and articulata,
Receptive like a receptaculitid,
Verbal in the classroom but, quiet in quiet water.
Has free cheeks and simple pygidium chin,
Curving ears are outlined by shell lines.
Marginal furrows have formed from age.
Short hair consists of primibrachials
And secundibrachials.

Nose peaks at the apex as do gastropods.
Is a siphuncle with hyponomic sinuses.
Breathes through hydrospire pores,
Has two pleural lobes and one axial.
Lung looks like a leucon.

Brain is housed in a tegmen,
Connected by nerve trunks to a spinal cord.
Soaks up knowledge like a porifera.
Encrusting colony attached to a cephalon,
Containing folds and sulci.
Arms and calyx form a crown,
That rests on his head.

Though generally benthic,
Preferring carpeting to tiled floors,
He becomes nectonic in swimming pools.
Arteries are full of red seawater.

Arms extend out of actinal furrows,
Legs project from notches.
Has winged shoulders like Spiriferida,
And a long hinge line,
A nema hand and rhamose fingers.
Is mainly bilaterally symmetrical,
But has radial fingers and toes.
Body has internal supports,
Made of calcite discs and spicules.

Truth flows from a lipped aperture,
Whose tongue is curved like nipponites.
Tongue becomes a radula to eat plants,
Is at other times a lophophore.
A sophisticated jaw apparatus is used,
For eating sea cucumbers in salad.
Food is stored on the littoral shelf,
Gastrozoid, always eating.
Has two hinges which open a bivalve mouth.
Lateral teeth are on the sides,
Isodonts are in the front.
Dines out like a dinoflagellate,
With sand dollars in his pocket.
Is known as a selective feeder in restaurants.
When he wants to feed,
He stretches his arm system out,

Arms deposit food in a mouth,
To be propelled down a groove.
Is digested then distributed,
Throughout the cytoplasm.

Has friendly trilobite eyes,
With complex facets,
That are coiled like a nautiloid,
Into different pastel-colored zones.
Ordinary and miliary tubercles cover his face;
He shaves the ciliated spines.
Autopores and mesopores add decor.
A septal neck supports his high authentic
Social profile.

Prefers a sessile life,
To the agitation of a department.
Everytime he tries to implant,
Someone pulls him out to do work.
At home he listens to the radio,
Like a radiolarian.
Prefers sheltered hidden offices
To classrooms.
Would be happy moving up and down
A burrow for the rest of his life,
But we make him teach.

The mantle secretes a shell,
For this introverted brachiopod.
Comes out for class at 11:15,
Runs back in at 12:15.
Shell opens by didductors;
Closes by adductors.
Is worn in dorsal and ventral positions,
By a vagile walker with tube feet.
He can change locomotion,
But generally moves with front forward.
Legs divide into oscicles,
Whose ridges and grooves fit well together.
Are shaped like straight ammonoids.

His biconvex body could fit well,
A brachiopod description,
But he has well-developed sense organs.
The weight of this body
Would cause it to sink in mud.
Is stable in shape so won't topple over.
Is well published like Productidina,
Studies attached to a desk by a pedicle.
When Orthida and Pentamerida died,
He prospered.
Had forty-nine families for relatives,
Then all but seven died.
Was rare in Triassic; Recovered in Jurassic.
Little affected by the Permean extinction,
As had the best aspects of all creatures.
First appeared in Cambrian.
Then peaked in Devonian.
Still gives lectures at present.

Down the halls of the geology department,
This fossil walks with class,
Extended mainly in a dorsal ventral direction.
Is somewhere up in the phyllum post-chordata,
Though has some of the characteristics,
Of Kingdom Metazoa.
Multicelled eucaryote,
Remember your ancestor was procaryote,
And your history Paleontology.
One of a billion creatures,
Known to have lived.

Fussy about turbidity,
He waits for the air to clear,
To begin his classic peformance.
The stage is set for invertebrates,
By a man fated to teach the subject.
He feels for them with a great heart;
Each in history has played a unique part.
Each thought itself the center,
Till it became extinct.

A Poem For My Geology Advisor, Dr. Leo Hall

You're gone from here,
Over to the energy side,
Where geologists map
Rock formations,
Free of flaws.

The rocks you see now,
Shimmer and shine,
In divine light.
Free of dust,
To hide their shades.

I was sad to hear,
You would never again appear
At your office.
It's lonely when one's advisor
Goes over to the other side.

I remember when,
You helped me to collect,
Some rock specimens to study.
All of my slides,
You scrutinized carefully,
Under a microscope.
I was grateful when,
You checked all of my numbers,
For error.
The result wouldn't have been
The same.
And if they ask me
If you cared,
I will say you did.
You made me a geologist.
You did.

A Poem for Gloria Radkey

There are mountains rising in the sky.
One of their peaks should bear your name.
There are rock formations forming every day.
One of the best should wear your name.

We were both in graduate school once.
Your desk stood across from mine.
You worked very hard,
Hoping to teach someday at Smith.

Your voice was sweet as an angels.
I heard it many times.
Flowers were often sent to you by admirers,
Though none reached my desk.

Then came a day when I was told,
Gloria would not be in the office anymore.
A car had entered her lane,
And took her life.
Someone an angel would have picked.
Was gone.

I will never understand,
Why somebody as good as you
Died so young.

I hope an angel grabbed you then,
And took you to the heavens.
I hope that you are studying now,
Rocks in the sky.

R. Bharath

Quick as a wit, generous as a bank,
For his infinite virtues we thank.
A smile for the ladies, just say please.
At your disposal, please don't tease.

Ruled the police for two thousand miles,
Was driven in a limousine like a king.
And justice to the Indians he did bring.
Although he didn't look the part,
With a tiny pygmy body,
And an enormous loving heart.
Frail delicate frame,
Housed great stores of justice inside.
Criminals loved him for he was forgiving,
Saw through gentle eyes that were wise.

Distributed food for a while,
As an agent of the govenment.
Directed the agricultural department.
Then as desire for knowledge gnawed,
Gave up security and fame,
To begin an academic game.

Who can this be?
Mr. Heebe-jeebe,
The incomparable R. Bharath,
Scholar, teacher, diplomat.
What hallowed meanings,
Do these words hold?
For a man who began a doctorate,
As a thirty-six year old.

None can compare, you see,
With the charm of his company,
Veritable character, personality.
R. Bharath, his followers will shout,
"Where have you gone out?"
Far from our eyes,
But not from our heart.
R. Bharath, R. Bharath, where can you be?
"Teaching new students," said he!

There wasn't more respectable a man.
Kept all his promises; was free of vices.
A true Brahmin, this Brahmaputra,
Patterning acts by perfection.
Forgot about himself.
The self-denying midget,
Cared for others,
Like they were his own.
Celibate man with so many children.
Father of everyone uncared for.

Let me describe the face of this great man,
So you might see him better.
Fuzzy hair cut short, sweet smile.
Eyes, two clear pools,
Reflect the image of his friends.
Soft brown like those of a deer,
Sharp as an owl.

Oxford professor in tennis shorts white,
Speaking only what was proper and right.
Comforting wounded hearts till midnight.
Gentleman in the highest sense.
Showing compassion without recompense.
Whatever your pleasure,
Whatever your bidding,
Have some tea while you are sitting.

Beans and potatoes for the stomach,
Scrabble for the head,
Slept on a cot that fell apart,
While in bed.
Served coffee for the social occasion,
Drank vodka in moderation.

Read for pleasure,
A hundred books on his floor.
Lamp without a cover,
For a philosophy book lover.
At peace with the universe,
In harmony with people,
Guided by reasoned intellect.

High up in a tree,
Tasting fruits of knowledge,
Throwing apples down to students,
Afraid to climb,
To those lonely heights.
So much knowledge in his head,
From staying there so long.
Truth must have struck that brain,
Many times.

Time nor distance shall ever
Dim our memories of R.B.
Clear as the afternoon sky,
You move, said he!

A Geologic Poem for Dr. Saul

Many atoms joined to make Dr. Saul,
As atoms do to form the biggest docs of all.
A brain he has that inspires,
Full of gems like rubies, topaz and sapphires.
His quartz cranial case is large and well-bound,
To hold the crystal thoughts he's formed.

A brilliant luster has this specimen.
He conducts his electrons well; they call him a gentleman.
With metallic charm he handles all.
He attends to the cares of the meek and small.
Less noble metals (like iron) he'll cure to be sure.
No vein of pyrite runs through his ore.

This remarkable man is justly called noble.
He resists oxidation and undesired reactions.
He answers pleas for medical actions.

He has primary minerals and accessory minerals,
When most others don't have necessary minerals.
Consolidated tuff and boring stuff,
With minds like volcanic bombs.
These mediocre agglomerates think aplomb.

The grand size of his thoughts,
Shows evidence of long schooling,
(Like magma that takes a while cooling).
Magma cooled slowly at great depths,
Forms big plutonic grains,
While that cooled quickly forms small brains.

You formed through diligent cogitation.
You happened through mindful intention.
Points of weakness in what was known,
Let you surface and be shown,
As a multi-talented crystal form.

27

Though I know that you are rich,
(In silica and alumina)
With depth you change to magnesia.
The quality of your textured manner,
The excellence of your moral character,
Reflects the mag"ma" from which you came.

If You Were My Father

If you were my father,
The ocean would surge through the door,
My mind washed of what was impure.
Waves would crash through the halls.
Go down the stairs like waterfalls,
Responding to universal calls.

The stormy sea that upsets me,
Would quiet and leave me free.
Crests would rise a thousand feet high.
To conflict I would say bye bye.

The Atlantic Ocean, the Mediterranean Sea,
Would agree you'd be a good father to me.
They'd move in rhythm to a daughterly breeze,
Unable to freeze.

Glaciers would melt.
Waters would cover the equatorial belt.
Gladness would be felt.
Rain would pour across an unhappy shore.
Glad to feel secure.
Of your paternal love, I could be sure.

From the depths that have brought demise,
The crust would rise.
Fresh layers exposed,
As forces in the rocks no longer opposed.
Giant waves would run for miles,
Before they overlapped in piles.
To greet them would be smiles.

And would you be a father to me?
And would you help to set me free?
Or alone and wishing must I always be.

If with this plea you did abide,
Mental treasure chests would open wide,
Spill jeweled thoughts at your side.
Beneath disturbed sands they presently hide.

Enamoured and blessed, I would feel,
Finally to have a father whose love was real.
Open wounds would heal.

A Geologic Poem About An Ivy League College

May I let Gabbro speak to you,
To tell you how I feel?
"It's like rockslides fell upon her,
Covering her Ivy League ideal.
For the past few months, amidst that debris,
She has dwelt."

To relate to a rock would be more endearing,
Than to one of these professors uncaring.
They smile like galena,
Put me inside their intellectual arena.
For a treat, compare me with their student elite.
(To some polished specimen that doesn't look so bright).
Their eyes shine like magnetite.

They all seem to know what is wrong and right;
Most of their rules seem so trite.
And their enamoured pupils seem as though
They were not yet touched by divine light.

Making me feel like fool's gold,
And showing me false warmth that in fact feels cold.

When I think of intellectual pursuits,
I wanted to be trying,
I return to the nights spent sighing.
And when I reflect on meaningful things
I wanted to do here,
I see past the cold, bold and old,
To the truth that could unfold.
(Like a nugget in a bad lode.)

It's lonely here,
Among people who don't speak but smile.
Their empathy is quick to cleave,
Makes me await the chance to leave.

In classes and parties they display their facets.
(Cause me to admire their variegated aspects).
Then suddenly when I've been won,
Through their intellectual fun,
One of those sides is used,
As part of a game,
To hurt outsiders who have came.

And C's in Organic add to the pain.
They seem to fall with the rain.
With brass buckets I collect them,
And put them in my pockets.
They form a fine organic veneer,
Upon my career.

Vincent Portrait I

Face is an impressionistic painting,
Containing airy strokes of pink shades,
Bordered by a hairy frame.
Look is of a Roman emperor,
Who had witnessed many battles,
Or of a Greek professor,
Who had mastered his subjects.

Eyes are touches of azure blue and green,
From a deep tropical sea.
Possess the wisdom of a wizard,
The knowledge of a scholar.
They gaze from an erudite plane,
Down on ordinary people.
Ageless eyes transcend to another world,
Outside this false universe,
Where people are honest, relationships timeless.
The best of virtues are held within them.

Golden curls stream down his neck,
In regular waves.
They join to form a widow's peak,
Near the crown of his head.
Sculptured lips are dark pink,
Against a bronze skin background.
They speak the truth,
Heedless of personal consequence.
Precocious wrinkles are engraved,
Upon a deepset forehead.
Two sweet dimples are imprints
Of an artist's thumbs,
At the sides of a crazy smile.

Neck has strong lines,
Like the base of the Rodin sculpture.
Body is built like a macho statue,
From lifting patients,
When they fall out of bed.
Has artistic contours and a sloping belly,
From being fed well in fancy restaurants.

Narcissus would have been proud of this creature,
Who spends so much time embellishing features,
In a full-length mirror.
Skilled fingers are artsy and pudgy.
Full cheeks are rosy and smudgy.

Vincent, a patient needs a respirator.
Bring some blood and plasma.
A broom to clean the floor.
We'll let you do the chore.
Vincent, we don't know what to do,
So you can take control.
The M.D.s will step aside,
As soon as you arrive.

Vincent, your brilliance shines,
Like silver plates on a knight's armour.
Wields a lancet tongue sharp with truth,
Directed at villainous targets,
Like medical doctors and supervisors.
Protects nurses from ignorance and abuse
Of the medical profession.

Appears gentle until he sees
Incompetence,
Then madness flashes in his eyes.
You love to preserve life.
When doctors try to pull respirators,
You replug them.
Ignore lazy excuses in the process.

Professional in the daytime,
Upholding high ethics in city hospitals.
You lose formality at night
On a bed with satin sheets,
Indulging in frank desire.
You kiss behind a forbidden door,
Where the stars cannot penetrate,
And the moon cannot enter.

Enjoy clubs and bright lights at night,
A chance to meet good people,
And share a leisurely drink.
Dance in step to the disco beat,
Till you tire in the heat,
Then return home to sleep.
Vincent, you are my best most cherished friend.
Though on separate paths of life we trend,
In the end we will meet again, in the end........
As all good men eternity spend.

Vincent Portrait II

Leonardo Da Vinci would have been proud,
Of this masterpiece dressed each day like Jason,
In a different colored fleece.
Endowed by a manly muscled frame,
Wearing only clothes bearing a designer's name.
Italian wavy hair was styled by a master barber
To meet the latest requirements of men's fashion.
Fingers placed each hair just so.
Was combed exactly over his ears to flow.
That golden widow's peak, bleached by the sun,
Blends in with browns, brushed back
Around the sides of his head.
Bends upwards at the base, around his smiling face.

An artist's inward pointing brow,
Richly painted dark brown,
Lowered, converging outwards in a plane,
To show he means it.
Penetrating lines abstruse in the daylight,
Belong in the night.
See from another dimension,
Raised above this horizon.

Ruddy face, upheld by a neck
In principled pose,
Possesses a prominent Roman nose.
Walks with dignified carried shoulders
That give an impression mature and older.
Warm eyes are full of love,
Intensity and sincerity,
They laugh as you stare at him seriously.

Venus blessed you with beauty,
Unusual and supernatural,
Only the authentic could see,
So only the true and handsome
Would flock to thee.
In any kind of weather,
Looks S & M in leather.

Ten gold rings mean Vincent is loved.
If something happens, at least he has his jewels.
A diamond bracelet covered with his initials,
Gold chains and bands of various sizes,
And thicknesses.
At least he isn't lonely with his riches.
Of all of the treasures in his collection,
The most precious by far,
Are two jeweled eyes that are genuine.
Only the wealthy can afford to love
My friend Vincent.

Self-Portrait

Inclined hornblende eyebrows,
Rest above brown crystal eyes.
Recumbent roman nose,
Sits upon a feldspar face.
Laughter flows from a geode mouth,
Lined with white quartz teeth.

Dark plagioclase hair,
Flows over granite shoulders.
Short plagioclase bangs,
Hang over a granite forehead.

There is romance in these eyes,
More than will be had in this lifetime.
Perhaps a hundred years from now,
A close encounter will occur,
With someone supernatural.
Someone of past history,
Will live again,
To love me for eternity.

A hallow granite heart,
Is lined with precious minerals.
A folded igneous brain,
Is full of pegmatitic thoughts.

An invisible gold crown,
Containing sapphires and emeralds,
Rests upon the head.
A dark sapphire shirt,
Is tucked inside a pair of topaz slacks.
Tourmaline black shoes,
Are worn with matching socks.

There is too much rock on this frame.
My stomach once a peneplane,
Has since become a dome.
Too many slabs hang from my arms,
Too many plates move within my legs.
My poor tired feet
Can barely hold the weight.
Soon I will diet,
So my friends will become quiet.
Or everywhere I step,
The earth will be upset.

Robert Stanton

Wavy black hair, wizened by silver streaked,
Boyish-looking face, poetically shaped.
Intense brown eyes reach out of glasses,
To touch Reality's fine lace.

A just mind seeks ideals; a gifted artist feels.
Through fingers that quiver,
With talent and love.
Emotions appear on paper shaped;
Thoughts are patterned and placed.
Images splash across blue lines,
Expressing meanings fine.

Light from the sky sees through his eyes.
Intelligence thinks in a hideous brain.
A little demon with a psychotic imagination,
Walks on campus and reads in libraries,
Possessed with hideous creations,
Like poems and short stories.

A muse speaks to him amused.
Because of its presence,
He has to write.
Thinks he wills to, loves to,
But is inspired to print
What's in that brain!

Energy flashes through eyes,
When a muse's lightning strikes.
Feeling rains over countless neurons,
Hypertrophied through use.
Fattened cell bodies secrete short stories.
Created by Robert with help
From celestial heat.

For the sake of Poetry,
A universe is digested.
As people eat peaches and plums,
Stanzas are synthesized
From pieces engulfed.

Words fall from trees,
Shaken, but helped by a surreal breeze.
Truth is picked from grass
As someone does sneeze.

He is ten years old today,
Running through holes in domes,
Playing in his past.
Regressed, this man writes
Children's stories.
Then returns to an adult,
So no one will know,
The story was written by a minor
Who couldn't be paid.

Books and stories whirl through his head.
If only he could stop them,
He'd be rich indeed.
His id is saddled in when he writes,
It can only run so far,
Before the conscious grabs it,
To use its energy for works.
Afraid to be an id for long,
He structures stories,
Then imagines in them.

Robert wears a poet's crown,
Adorned with metaphors and similes,
Worth to him what diamonds and rubies
Are to jewelers.
Collects lines for pleasure.
The worth of one poem,
Can have no measure.

His trunk's a tree; artist fingers leaves,
Arms are covered with striped blue sleeves.
An outlaw in trouble with relatives and friends,
For not possessing values right.
For wanting to write.

Like Can't See they live,
In a fog in a bog.
Realize little meaning, dreaming.
Give comments that bite,
At soft petals of a poet's heart.

Through a rhythmic voice,
The wind speaks.
Standing Earth writes,
In touch with elements and worth.

A madman roams free in his house,
Where sinks make love to bathtubs,
And furniture feels.
Needle people live there,
White finger and Face.

On his hands are transparent knight gloves,
He wears while riding a stallion,
Fenced in his backyard.
He could have ruled a country once,
In medieval times,
Permitting people to become what they wanted,
Removed from obstacles,
If one of the kings would have let him then,
And if he was around.
At least a knight, full of romance and passion,
Clothed in silver shining armour,
Peacefully carrying a heavy rapier.
His charming manner
Would have made a maiden elope,
Like Pomona when Vertumnus tried his best.

She and I in love,
On the last night in April,
When she tried to repress my writing,
And they try too.
But distant stars will always shine for me,
As my senses are open.
Will make a great rock formation someday,
The kind the Earth would love to swallow up.
With distinctive polished features,
Deeply weathered fissures,
From willed suffering a poet's pain.

Rocks lie still beneath his feet,
Won't slip and slide,
Though they can move also,
Under volition.
Out of respect, they let him stay
So he can write poems another day.

The Professor in the Elevator

I met a professor the other day
—In an elevator.
He was handsome and reserved,
With a black goatee and well-built body.

He looked my way with a man's looks,
As I held my chemistry books.
Afraid to respond aloud, I stood cowardly.
His shoulders were broad and held proudly,
As was his head.

It was lonely till he arrived,
And waited with us
For that elevator to come down.
Doors to open wide to let us inside.
Like waiting for Godot; it was so slow.

I stood with a girl,
Announced it was too early for class,
When what I really wanted was,
A romance with this professor from the elevator.
To share a glass of wine,
At the top of the campus center,
Looking out at buildings touched by winter.

He really surprised me suddenly to appear,
Out of mid-air
Made me happy to be there,
Waiting for that blasted elevator.
My heart moved towards his as he said "hello."
Those dark absorbing eyes took me in.
It felt good to be inside his mind.
His eyes glittered and mesmerized me,
As he held me in his mind.

Those arms looked so strong,
And felt warm from the distance.
Could tell he'd made a good lover,
For someone like me.
His foreign face was like one of those
I always wanted.

Didn't know which department he was from,
Math or physics probably, though perhaps astronomy.
The G.R.T. encompasses several varieties,
So one cannot tell by visible qualities.
He looked Italian or Greek.
I asked his name.
He said "No speak anglais.
Am italiano."
I said "Fine."

Wanted to ask if he'd like to spend some time,
At least to have coffee at the U. Mass Café.
Then there'd be a chance
To convince him we should go to dance.
That would be the start of inevitable romance,
Between this foreigner and professor conqueror.

We'd be so good together.
Why did I have to wait,
For him to state, "We should go out with each other"
—Of course we should date.

Those eyes reflected like a deep mirror.
Let me see myself within them plainly,
As someone who needed a man who was manly.
Then we merged, as my eyes met his,
And his met mine.
My nose pressed next to his,
As his face moved over mine.
We held each other closely, solidly,
In my mind.

As he stood there waiting patiently,
For the doors to open,
I held his hand with one of mine,
His child with the other.
Walked along the sidewalk of Main Street
Through the Center of Amherst.

I felt happy with him near me and complete.
To have him for a husband would be a treat.
He could teach his class and I mine.
Wait for him to come home till nine.

I asked him since he was Italian,
Did he watch "The Godfather."
He said it's not really like that
And, if I could think that way,
Probably he wouldn't get tenure.

Said he liked me, had watched me for some time,
But even I had one fault, maybe more.
Couldn't marry me blindly since he wasn't sure.
He would give me a chance, if he wasn't going back,
But since he was he couldn't,
Or would disappoint me, break my heart,
Have to get rid of me before he packed.

The door opened at his floor,
Beneath the one I was waiting for.
He left to do his professor chores,
Never to know the world I had created for us.

Professor Rowell of the Chemistry Department

Catalyst for the learning process,
You lower the activation energy
Required for learning.
Your energy overcomes the barrier.
Cause reactions to occur in minds,
Till you leave unused,
At the semester's end.

Mature, wise teacher; respected leader,
Young chemists follow.
Integrated personality,
Differentiated from other members,
Of the U. Mass. faculty.
Independent variable,
In the midst of dependent variables.
Undergraduates look up to you,
As a reference state.

One of the better combinations,
To have formed spontaneously,
Mr. Physical Chemistry.
Your creation was the product
Of many reactions.
You are well-constructed chemistry.
A partial derivative of both,
Your mother and father.
Born in an initial state;
Now an intermediate stage,
Along the road of life.

At low enough pressure
Your atoms would act independently,
Dissipating as a vapour in air.
Your chaos at room temperature
Isn't as bad as it would be
At high temperature.

A man of first order on the surface,
Complex with depth.
So deep that he has phases within phases.
The driving force for your reactions,
On a human level is to increase warmth and order.
On a molecular level is to decrease enthalpy,
And increase entropy.

Maintains a steady state under stress,
While most others
Are thrown out of equilibrium.
Active mass,
You effect equilibria of people,
With your concentrated being.

Walks down the halls,
With slow rate-determining steps,
Scattering light with his feet,
Splitting it into several wavelengths.

Enters the room with the right energy,
Orientation of attitudes,
For effective interaction.
There is zero order till he arrives.
Suddenly the atmosphere changes to first order.
By the end of the lecture it is tenth order.

Cohesive forces fill the classroom
When he teaches.
Man of great enthalpy,
Heated by divine flames,
Warms the air with exothermic reactivity.

Wears a fundamental expression
That is sincere.
Disposition has an unusual composition,
With no equivalent.
Consistent personality defies,
The Law of Entropy.
Face is a fated form,
Patterned like a gel to fit a mould.
Is happy under standard conditions.

Eyes shine like gold suns.
Send out intense beams of light,
That radiate throughout the classroom.
Voice travels through space,
Like pleasant sound through air.
Tones are of a melody in harmony.
Speaks the truth before us,
With certain approximations and assumptions.

Brain is a favorable free energy
Surface for knowledge,
Absorbed like heat by an endergonic reaction.
This model of electrochemistry,
Has a large EMF potential.
Neurons try to do their selective best,
So not all data will pass the test.
Mind consists of pure substances
That seek ideal solutions to problems.

Says he likes to think like a molecule,
But how does a molecule think?
Though molecules have the potential for thinking,
And actualize this capacity as man,
This requires millions.
What can a single molecule do besides motion?
You think instead as many molecules,
Which have potential for morality,
As you are a man of principles.

Have high academic potential,
As a metaphysical chemical.
Low activity constant doesn't deviate
Significantly from ideal.
Behave as well in concentrated situations,
As in dilute, always considerate and polite.
Thermodynamics and kinetics favour,
The best human relations.

Constructively tries to direct,
Most heat into useful work.
Has a large rate constant,
In the laboratory.
Works too quickly for heat flows
To keep up with.
Can withstand great pressure.
The larger the P external,
The more work he can do.

Surface tension exists when he gives quizzes.
Makes exams easy,
To not give students vapor-pressure depression.

Is often busy in his office.
When work tapers,
Enjoys his relaxation time.
If a student has problems,
His mind becomes turbulent.

Tries to solve the matter logically,
Emotionally becomes a soothing solvent.
Polar part dissolves listening to sad stories.
Supportive of students' ambitions,
Never gives activated complexes.
Delta G is negative but he is positive.

Has several degrees of freedom,
According to Gibbs' Phase Rule.
Still takes some orders,
Like the rest of us.
May be reduced by the chairman,
But may oxidize graduate students.
Charges up those who need motivation,
Like a battery.
Seems a rare gas crystal,
Condensed from ether,
As he is a perfect teacher.

Professor Richard Stein

Richard Stein is the King,
All the Chemists sing.
The best of chemical reactions.
To the court he brings.
A Father of polymer science
Is this brilliant man.
Shout it down the halls.
Let it ring off the walls.
A crown on his head.
In publishings he is far ahead.
Two hundred papers or more,
In journals throughout the world.

He stands as a polymer six feet tall.
The most fit to rule of all.
Neurons are linked in a gold chain,
Inside his brain.
In character there is only one this high.
Consciousness soars across the sky.
His soul is from heaven;
That's why we need one, not seven.

The crown should be made
Of the noblest of atoms,
Arranged in jeweled patterns,
Reflecting light in all directions,
Covering the entire spectrum.
He should be cloaked,
In a polysynthetic robe,
Of royal blue velvet,
To match his eyes.

Stern eyes are wise,
Able to penetrate disguise.
Seem focused in attention and intense,
Devoid of any pretense.
Sincere smile runs from ear to ear.
Has the beginnings of dimples.
Pointed chin, raised in distinction,
Rests on an arc-shaped base.
Big ears bounce about his face.
Forehead is deepset with mature wrinkles.

Wears a traditional gray-striped suit
And conservative tie.
Walks distinguished by,
Shifting his weight
With a merry gait.
A paper always in his hand,
As he walks about the land.

A just man, compassionate and kind,
Patient with the unpublished
And undeveloped.
Subjects sit and wait,
For research problems to be distributed.
Recognizes those deserving,
Is reserved in judgment
For those still earning.
Encourages the quiet and meek,
Is eloquent and truthful,
When he speaks.
A rare treat,
To hear an individual who has done
So many feats.

Holds his head regally high,
Honorably and humbly,
His majesty.
Has a joint appointment,
In two departments.
Two offices for thrones,
With royal phones.
Secretaries type decrees happily,
Grad students kneel in respect loyally.
Listen attentively, obey willingly,
For he's the best they've seen.

Believes in democracy,
But we prefer him as King.
Dream on...
But who could ask for better.
Hope for more perfection would fester,
As a request with no answer.
For there is no one out there
Who is greater.

Francis

Distinguished Francis, face scholarly shaped,
Moulded distinctly in Oxford's special design,
Interior complicated, not easy to define,
Well kept and cultured like fine wine.
Blondish brown hair that sits at various angles in the air.
(Sometimes well-combed, but who in physics cares).

His eyebrows are intense, without compare.
His eyes are sapphire blue and rare.
Intent they appear and content,
To peer at those who are beautiful and fair.
Unusual eyes deeply sincere and dear,
Sweetly innocent though it is clear,
Behind them is a man always there.

Accomplished to an academic T.
Exactly so he solves his physics equations.
Gives all the correct mathematical derivations.
Decides which articles will make journals.
Attends those conferences that are reasonably seasonal.
Leads Linus Pauling around the floor,
Talks with C.N. Yang as he enters the main door.
(Who could ask for status more?)

At home he cares for those who need his love.
I fit in his lap like a little hand,
In a moderate-sized glove.
We sit together on his plush, brown couch,
Looking past the patio to the stars.
His physics book lies in the bookcase.
Francis indeed is intellectually splendid—
An academic prize who is in many ways wise.
With speech like Shakespeare, eloquent and true,
It's no wonder I should care for you.

President Reagan

The President's face is kind and great,
From meeting with the heads of state.
The President's eyes are sincere and humane,
Men around him do principles gain.
Across this handsome timeless face,
Flow lines with grace.

Out of a world of movie screens
Came a President who would walk
With Kings and Queens.
In his life he went very far,
Expressing himself as a star.

Wise lines carve an intelligent face,
Free of prejudice based on race.
He bears respect for American ideals,
Sipping champagne and eating fancy meals.
While cattle are rounded up on a ranch,
He consults with the senate branch.

In a white cardigan, a TV director
Hands out parts to people in movies.
Hollywood made this face,
A Disneyworld comedy.
An actor's romance with people,
Out on the world's great stage.
A big part in a play that changes everyday,
Features people from all walks of life,
Playing individual roles.

He decides the plot of the U.S.A.
The Kremlin watches with dismay,
As the Head of the Actors Guild
Has his way.
Men in uniforms obey, actors costumes sway.

A romantic face has sweet blue eyes,
Which look people in the eye.
A crest of brown hair flows back,
Over his neck in a wave.
Focused eyebrows rest above penetrating eyes,
That question and analyze.

His long black suit has tails in the back.
His plain white shirt has a tie in the front.
A handkerchief extends from a pocket over his chest,
So he will look his best.
Shiny black shoes are worn with black socks.

He sits carefully listening to representatives,
Hearing the cases of all people.
Decides the cure for each business.
Tries to solve the problems of the rich and poor,
The extravagant and the miserable.

Money here, money there, throw some money everywhere.
Some for Asia, some for Africa, some for Guatemala.
Some for me, some for you, save some money too.
Wonder why you aren't tired of lending money.
That isn't paid back.

This man is very sweet,
So every country wants something from him.
And his face shows such love,
That everyone wants him in their land.
Over here, over there, his plane goes everywhere.

Security people follow at his side,
As people swarm to greet him.
He shakes a hand and signs an autograph,
For people who appreciate him.

All alone his mind must decide,
What to veto, what to approve,
Which thoughts are right,
Which thoughts are wrong.
Where to save a dollar,
Where to spend.

Advisors are fine, so is a wife.
Sometimes a man's kindness,
Is what ends conflict and strife.
A President's quill is a powerful pen.
His thinking must be sound,
As it strikes again and again.
Though there are people who enjoy
When countries fight,
A President must find peace within himself,
And spread it left and right.

R.D. Laing

Laing a Laing a Laing a Laing
The patients sang.
Schizophrenia's a trip.
I like to take an unconscious dip,
In a pool of images and sounds,
Of people I used to play around.

He's so outrageous; he's outlandish.
A king of psychotics galore.
Protecting their tumbling on the floor,
Object-throwing out the door,
Patterned finger movements to music,
Facial transformations
That express new varieties of emotions.
Indulging in books the way they think,
Living life on the brink.

We're all a bit demented,
By disturbed psyches cemented.
Madness is the best,
When put to the test.
When the id runs free,
Happy we be.

He's alone on the frontier,
On a high beam balancing
What is right.
Standing firm; trying not to shake.
Some wait for his fall,
But R.D Laing, free of doubt,
Is stable at that height,
With knees locked tight.
A happy expression sits on his face.

Few people care
About the truth he wears.
A philosopher's spiritual dress
Is hidden behind Existential
Worldly clothes.
You wear sneakers and a sweater,
When others wear distinguished suits.
Your neck from restraining ties
Must be free.
Jacket is never on straight.
Whispy brown hair flies wild
On windy days.

You smile uncontrolled at good jokes,
When some try to keep still.
You have a bottomless laughter.
When you laugh,
Your mouth drops to the ground,
Tongue rolls and flips over,
Eyes light up like two unmatched lamps.
Blink on and off for days,
Till the next joke comes,
Like a train to transport you
To another place in space.
Your neck twists around,
Wringing in rhythm
To the laughter.
Your hands like two drumsticks,
Beat up and down on your knees,
Fingers move in all directions,
Spastically.

R.D. Laing, when you walk,
You slide from side to side.
Legs round out like a skater,
Doing figure eights.—
A fine way to reach
Your destination.
Your back at times is bent,
Like the hunchback from Notre Dame.

When you talk,
It's like a schizophrenic spoke,
Sharing new and different meanings.
Find in their speech, patterns
Out of seeming nonsense.

An honest man;
His books a leisurely pleasure,
Full of meaning and worth,
Not demeaning experiences of those,
Society doesn't attribute positive worth.

Born into families of cruel birth,
That beat them and mistreat them,
These people try to create a world happy by
A voyage to a better place,
Then return to act it out.
Are placed in hospitals
If they shout,
Or fail to heed conventions somewhere.

And what right do people have
To give them stigmas,
Dementias?
Let's leave them to talk
With R.D. Laing,
About the profound.
He's a man to join the gang.
Sing insane songs when he's around.

He's the one we love,
With a face true and sincere,
There'll never be another
Like this brother—
Mother, he's real.

Normality was created
To keep each in his place,
So a psychiatrist could give doses,
With a respectable face.
Drugs have effects far from ideal.

Lock people inside a mad door
If they don't want to live,
Like the mediocrity, insensitively,
If they want to live unusually.

The mind can do anything, R.D. Laing,
You've got potential..
We can become anything we want,
With a thought or image.
You've not lost sight of this fact,
Illuminating minds of others blind.

You are great, R.D. Laing,
My idol evermore.
Enjoy your height,
But look with compassion
At ignorance left and right,
Of doctors beneath, out of light.

Help them R.D. Laing;
Give them treatment.
Don't be frustrated
By what they try to do to you.
For they know not what they do.

It's good from a distance,
To relate to you,
For I am a different person too.
Just one of the gang,
Headed by R.D. Laing.

Professions

Professions and their snide outrageous grin,
With their selection committees I can never win.
No matter how hard I try,
They always find reason to pass my application by.

Decorated with awards from universities here and there,
Transcripts filled with grades beyond compare,
Makes me think their sight isn't all there.

Unneeded professions, hypercritical,
Don't use criteria enough intellectual.
Creativity hardly matters to them,
When they decide who is to get in,
And toss the ones they don't like
In the rejection bin.
The ones they like are in accomplishments
Exceptionally thin.

Professions, why oh why,
Can't they see an individual such as me,
Accepted should be.

Deceptive the criteria they use,
Unreasoned how they choose.
Irrational phenomena causing catastromena.

The few competent members
Of the Medical Profession,
Cover mistakes of the incompetent,
Till they are beyond recognition.
Profess to possess humane impulses,
Which in fact they have not.

Why they act to block progress,
Toss aside the minds that really think,
Makes me want to throw my application
Over the brink.

Russell's Poem

I was hitching from Route Nine,
A blue-eyed man gave me a ride.
He wore a kind expression,
Which meant he cared for others.
The day was hot; the sun hurt my eyes
Before he left me inside.
A pale blue car simple and plain,
Had gone hundreds of thousands of miles,
In the fog and the rain.
Was driving around to pass the time
Before an appointment in Springfield,
To see how his stocks were trading,
When he spotted me waiting.

He looked like the man
Who once sold bicycles
In my neighborhood,
With that scooped-out space,
At the side of his face,
And lopsided way of posing.
That red nose showed scars,
From where a doctor cut.

He was a land surveyor with the talent
To find boundaries unnoticed by others.
They called him an Indian because of the fact,
He could walk through the forest for miles
Without a marker to trace his path.
Would return by use of an extra sense,
To his house by the woods of Bingham, Maine.
While we rode in his car he told me that
The time had come at last to begin
A new phase in life.
Free time he now wanted to spend,
Hunting and fishing,
In pure lakes and pristine forests.
Trips to Italy and Spain were planned,
As were visits to the states he had missed.

We got along quite well in discussion.
Like two rocks sitting together in a box,
Without a care in the world.
The rocks in my head resonated,
In tune with the conversation.
I aligned them in proper formation,
To absorb his many jokes and stories.

When we went to Aqua Vita for dinner,
He stood tall and lean,
Holding the door open,
While I stepped inside.
He showed pictures of his trips,
As we sipped wine.

Lines ran over the top of his chest,
The marks of an almost tragedy.
He said he was a lucky man
Who would have died many times,
Had he been any other.
Once from the cancer;
Once from the blood after.

He had been saved to teach others
That when they arrive
At the crossroads of life,
When either one acts or dies,
One ought to decide to live and to try.
For sometimes one must give up a limb,
An organ or whole set of muscles,
To prevent a disease from taking
The rest of the body.
He might have had to lose
A nose or his face as well,
If it had kept spreading.
But then he would be alive today,
With the replacement.

His eyes twinkled like blue star sapphires,
On a face plain and true.
Though he had fair white hair and a gentle air,
His eyes were most worthy of a line,
They were simply divine.

Fireworks were set off at nine-fifteen,
Starbursts filled the sky red, blue, and green.
We sat in the car by a farm,
In line with the site,
Staring wide-eyed with delight.
Flashing fireflies gave their own show.
Mosquitoes electrocuting themselves in masses,
On the electric fence,
Made flickering noises in the distance.
The warmth of his presence next to mine,
Made me enjoy passing the time.
As stimulating as that light show,
Were the thoughts we shared alone.

He took me to a park another day,
Where I watched him light up from youthful sparks,
The fountain of youth had found a place
In his mind; he spoke as though sixteen at times,
Blaming me for the cause.
Said how in his youth he had sorted out
What to believe and what to throw away,
How honesty was the best way.
I felt he was beside me that day,
In the human struggle.

It was good to meet a Rebel,
Who stood up for his beliefs,
In a gentlemanly manner.
He was supposed to be that way,
For he was related to Roger Williams.

We went to a party at Regina's,
Where I met a mean Nazi,
Who sawed a Jew in half
And bragged about it,
When the lights were dim,
And the glasses full.
He said "After all, when it is war
Either you kill them or they kill you.
So why not saw a Jew in two?"

He thought he too had had it bad,
When for fourteen days and fourteen nights
There was nothing to eat in sight.
A day before he crossed the Rhine,
It was red from the blood of Germans,
Who had been killed by Americans.
He had sent some Jews,
To their death in showers of gas,
And had spent some time
In a Russian camp.
I pitied this man who thought
He was going to Hell,
Because his actions showed,
He'd fit well there.

Russell hated the Nazi
For what he did,
But did not show it.
A gentleman will never show
That something is wrong,
When obviously there is.
I asked the Nazi if
He would have killed me too,
Had I been in Germany.
He said "No, because he liked me.
One does not kill what one likes."
I asked him if he could have
Used his conscience to not kill
A people who were innocent.

He said it wasn't his decision,
But someone higher who gave the order.
Soldiers followed or were shot.
When one was in the German army,
One did what one was told,
Or did not live to be very old.

A lesson that I learned from Russell
Was that there are still some men around,
Who will pick up fair ladies and rescue damsels.
The loneliness of most days is worth enduring,
To wait for the company of the amusing.
And through the ordeal of searching and screening,
There are still some golden moments to be had,
When a virtuous man passes through town.

A Poem for Taleb

Opal light shined the day,
God let you come my way.
A glass of club soda, lady's wine,
A face darkly featured in handsome foreign design.

Lebanon sent him so chance I could find,
Cross deserts and lands full of mid-east fruit.
A Ph.D. and fate led you to me,
At a night club along a Boston route.

And did you think, Taleb,
With one look I would not know you.
Your goodness could not hide,
Though the setting was one that virtue tried.

The smoke and wine did not affect your mind,
Nor was your parents' upbringing left behind.
All of the enamour of your foreign manner
Left me to think of amour,
And to hope you could be someone
Whom I could adore.

Indeed, I would have crossed any shore
In search of a man with virtues, many and sure,
Of character rare as mid-east jewels,
And dark eyes that shined like intelligent pools.

The love that comes from a man as good as this,
Must surely be bliss.
Did Taleb not on his first night,
Give me a delightful kiss?

Robert As I Knew Him

Robert was tall, from a world duplex,
A center of great forces complex.
At times an angel white,
Doing and speaking what was right.
Other times committing acts impulsive,
Black as night.
Congenial one moment, asocial the next,
But Robert tried to do his best.

Robert, the boy with the high I.Q.,
Remember the work you did not do.
You little genius, you.

His family treated him meanly,
That's why he didn't act well actually.
Impulses of all sorts filled his eyes,
As he checked them, learning to be wise.

With a thought could become a child.
Voice would squeak youthfully,
Muscles would grow sinewy.
With a thought could regulate the heartbeat,
By imagining a sight that was a treat,
Would take great exertion to return,
From six years old to eighteen years.

Robert had the potential of a giant.
In anything touched, might be brilliant.
Able to read a page a second, a book an hour.
To no one did he ever cower.
Robert was not afraid to speak,
With a brain full of knowledge.
Discussed Freud and Einstein eagerly,
As he now discusses law,
Flipped theories in his mind flexibly.

Robert was a gentle soul who wished only to defend,
Poor people whose judgment the law had bent.
—Those who knew the wrong and chose it,
He defended a few,
As they deserved a fair trial too.

Compared with other men,
Robert had alot of class.
In taxis we drove around.
The finest restaurants he picked in town.
Always carried a thick wallet,
Spent all of what was in his pocket,
Promised the world in a moment.

In high school, Robert only thought of me,
Waited outside classes till I was free.
Walked hand in hand loyally down the halls,
Did not look at other girls.
Gave sweet kisses many,
As we embraced on the stairs.

Robert was too handsome for so much loyalty.
I wondered why he chose to love me.
That's why I didn't stay with you.
To remake those moments what wouldn't I do.
To care for you as you should have been cared for,
Stay in your arms and love you evermore.
Would all be blissful sure.
But you are not mine anymore,
And others wait outside the door.

Second Best

Think not it is you who leaves me warm,
But my love of him for whom I wait.
I warned that I loved.
His dark blue eyes will always be there,
Sparkling, enticing me to his side.
Still I may not have,
Though I will to have and I do wait.
You I will keep in my pocket.
At him I gaze like a star,
To worship high on some pedestal.
How many light years are you free?

Introversion

If love could be made sure by a promise,
How fast I would swear—but it can't.
One moment I love, the next I like.
A single word, carelessly placed,
Can turn off my love and crush my desire.

How vulnerable my feelings are.
How insecure I am,
To let one word end everything
I've felt for you.

Fickle my love is,
So easily turned back.
But why should I risk my love on you,
When on myself I can rely?

The Pain You Caused

The words you spoke stirred once covered hurt.
Exposed my pain in streaks,
That flowed through my arms.

You uncovered what took years to settle,
On my mind's grey floor.
Each disappointment had found its place,
Between grains of frustration,
And they were, oh so quiet, forgotten there.

Till you came along and stirred the mud.
You spoke the truth that made my mouth lie low.
Now I fear my sea of peace is forever dammed.
My tide of self-love is held back
By the wall of truth.

My anger is rising in a wave of tears,
Crashing loudly on my old beliefs.
My vision is dimming.
I can no longer see
The face I thought so perfect.

A Change of Tide

The tide is changing.
My love has begun to ebb,
Carrying all of its bubbling sensation
Back to the sea.

It no longer advances
In sudden waves of energy,
Crashing down society's illusions,
And building its own truth with the remains.

I'm leaving the beach as it has lain,
As it has been ordained to lie.
I'm receding and the sand is holding firm,
Warmed by the sun and dried by time.

The waves tore apart the sand castle,
We had built together,
And left a moat for me to cry in.
Someone else's love will withstand
The stresses mine could not bear.

The End of My Love

My love is folding again,
Tightening inside of me.
I'm me again, not us.

You've wrecked everything,
There was for you inside of me.
There is nothing left—
But a vacuum.

No More Geniuses

I thought I wanted a genius once,
They're in style, you know,
And hard to find.
But when I found one and saw,
How unstable he was,
And how conceited he was,
I wished I hadn't met him.

Brilliant is now enough for me,
Benevolent modesty I want to see.
Someone not smart enough,
To become obsessed with his brain.
Yet someone bright enough,
To see me as I am.

Your Love

Your love and the blue sea,
Cool and wavy.
Lone birds fly in the sky,
Tweedle-deeing past my eye.
Hoping you don't pass me by.
I wonder if choppy seas can bend,
And your high tide can flow with mine.
If a fool moon washed me to your shore,
Would you love me evermore?
Sand bars and low hellos,
Muddy holes and blows.
The breeze lies and teases,
But it sometimes pleases.

Sunset

Come down angry torch,
Come down and cease to burn.

Down further, hot cherry,
My face is red as your flame.

Call it wondrous sunset,
This red curse?

Down. Down.
Flow through the ground.
Burning pest shine elsewhere.

The Wait

I waited as creases fell to the floor.
Sweat rose from my hands to the ceiling.
Old faces passed in a mist,
Of smoke and breath.
Cold it became, their faces froze in line.
I sat and watched to spend the time.
Wanting just a glimpse of you,
Your words to cause sparkles in my mind.
I waited in vain.
Slowly my feelings faded in pain,
And I lost sight of you within.
Alone I became, but less.

The Body

A lone corpse lay in an alley,
The flesh void of earthly color.
Swollen and livid was the face,
Overlain with sun-baked blood.
Old the body was, an eyeless rot.
Still, at sunset's start.

A shadow lay upon the corpse,
Hiding the pitted flesh of the arm.
A brick lay split beside the face,
Some bits still lodged inside the skull.

Outside the walls a demon ran,
Peddling his poison by the code of man.
Within the dark the corpse lay hid,
A product of his evil plan.

You, The Ocean And Me, The Air

You, the ocean, beneath the moon,
Deep and wonderful, full of hidden life.
Your polished aquamarine surface shines so well.
It sends moonbeams perfectly through me.
We mix at the edge of atmosphere and ocean-life,
Where water makes room for warming air.
I cause overturn in your world.
Your innermost currents respond to me.
I, the air and sometimes the wind,
Take my time to fill you within,
(With my love).
Sometimes my own conflicts and pressures,
Move me swiftly towards you—through you,
They find their answer,
Though gravity is their cause.
(I gravitate to you.)
As earth spins within, the moon and sun tease it out,
Sometimes pulling less and sometimes more,
As other planets affect the score,
Moving them towards conflictual poles—
That's part of the cause,
(Of why I'm attracted to you).
But then there's your irresistible surface,
The red tint of your gonuflagellates,
(Hair in ocean terms).
And then there's all that's teeming within,
Your gold-tinted fish, your lobsters, your crabs.
—Baby, you're quite a dish.

You and Your Folds and Faults

Evidence of ceaseless deformation is present
In all rocks and people,
No matter how young or old.
Some have been tilted, some fractured;
Others have been depressed or elevated, I'm told.

Past movement is recorded in rocks and minds.
Abrupt movements are there as are slow movements.
At times human ground has moved upward; at times downward,
Though erosion tries to hide the evidence,
And depressions fill in.

Some movements go on slowly, more or less continuously;
Others happen quickly, almost instantly.
Extensive movements of your crust,
Produced something I could hold on to.
Then deformation came produced by processes,
I could not stand up to.
Though deformation produced the magnificent forms
We find today,
It destroyed what I loved.

If only you could have been stable,
Like the ancient sages of the human field,
Or the oldest rocks of the Canadian Shield.

Before my eyes, you sank beneath an ocean.
As I tried to build upon the continent you showed me,
You became a restless area.

I should have predicted this.
Your face bore lines of unsettled times,
Gently tilted in places, folded into domes and basins.

I was happy when you seemed to be a constant plain.
I didn't want to see the rocks consisting you,
Had phenomena we call folds and faults.
I didn't want to look behind your pleasant surface,
Remembering that plains may be produced by distortions,
Like plateaus and mountain ranges.
The character that showed was due,
To resistance to another's cruel purpose.

Perhaps your folds were produced
While in a youthful plastic state.
Pardon me these folds were not sooner found.
I didn't want to know that they were around.
Sometimes bore-holes must be used to trace their bed.
Where to drill is verbally led.

When I chose to look, I saw not one fold but manifolds.
Sometimes these folds were broad,
Sometimes tight and narrow.
Sometimes they were tilted to one side,
Generally to your end.

Social processes creating your folds must have been slow,
So you could adjust to them without breaking.
But when these movements became of a nature
To break rocks and displace parts,
They produced a faulted feature.

The displacement that takes place along most faults
Isn't seen at the surface.
Even where the surface has been displaced,
Erosion may wear away its evidence.

You have strike-slip faults
And wrong-hand faults
Termed by the relative movements of your verbiage.
In normal faults, the hanging wall moves downward.
In thrust faults, the opposite occurs.
(Some of yours are thrust faults).

When I first came upon your joints,
I should have known what was beneath.
They ran vertically, horizontally, in almost any direction
(And at various angles).

When I saw sheeting,
I should have known what was beneath.
These patterns of horizontal joints occurred fairly close together,
But fooled me as they diminished underneath.

You, as an unconformity
Could have resulted from being raised,
As out of a sea and braised.
Then lowered and left to deposits of praise.
This action produces a surface
That separates younger less mature rocks
From older more mature rocks.

Time, quite important in this process,
Tells of much immaturity,
In relation to capacity for maturity.
Parallel beds lie on opposite sides,
In disconformity.

Weathering

The act of weathering wears people down,
Or else they would be forever around.
Were they allowed by eternal law to abound,
There would be no place for young rocks,
To sit on the ground.
When they tinker one at a time,
We are convinced the universe has committed a crime.
(Their bodies turn to gravels, solidified marvels).

By the time one is old enough to have life begin,
A layer of rock locks one within.
(Little arms dangle out holes at the sides).
Feelings lose their fundamental flavor.
They are taught to be exchanged like water.
One gives them out as barter,
To be carted by others away.

Products of erosional attacks
Are carried off despite cries from the child,
Who wants them back.
Erosion may be then so efficient,
As to make the child feel he is insufficient.
He feels imposed by those who want him exposed.

True sentiments of youth become sediments.
With less they experience anew.
Fresh thought is replaced by conventional thought,
Of what one ought and ought not do.

In intermediate stages while there is still some luster,
And the will has not all cleaved,
Innate goodness begins to leave.

Interesting remnants of once people may be seen.
They cover the campus green.
The most fractured of the troop,
Leads the demise of the rest of the group.
The most abundant people are already a part,
Of those who have little heart.

Debris is cleared away; more forms the next day.
Men cease to act true.
Act the way men are supposed to do.
(Rocks don't need love like people do.)
My heart makes up silts and sands.
It is crumpled by their hands.
It hardens and less often pardons.

Sandstone men are just sand grains attached to each other.
They seem held by cement together.
It's hard to have compassion,
To see they too are undergoing chemical reaction.
Hurt causes strain and pain.
It wears away at one's finer grain.
Insides dissolve and decompose
As we smile and pose.

Unwanted human boulders stand.
Their cracks wear over; rain covers their tears.
As alone they endure the hard years.
The digging of creatures brings more fragmentation.
Pressure causes relithification.
Cold words cause them to yearn to split,
(So that would be it).
The freeze-thawing cycle leaves one to feel,
Broken and unfit.

Old Age

Old age claws so fast,
With her fat gray paw.
Leaves her scratched rut,
O'er the face.

Tears the spirit from the corpse,
Once noble in its youth.
Sends it from the dried up scrap,
To somewhere of its worth.

Distorts the face,
Leaves heavy folds,
Of sagging fat,
That stretch the cheek.

Streaks hard silver,
Through once soft hair.
Cheapens the shine,
And dulls the strands.

Cripples the frame,
Which then must crawl,
With shaky limbs,
And hardened joints.

Leaves its prey,
To die in defeat,
With blinded eyes,
And lines worn deep.